W9-CNA-463

RELIGIONS OF THE WORLD

I Am Buddhist

❦ DANIEL P. QUINN ❦

The Rosen Publishing Group's
PowerKids Press™
New York

Published in 1996 by The Rosen Publishing Group, Inc.
29 East 21st Street, New York, NY 10010

First Edition

Book design: Erin McKenna and Kim Sonsky

Photo credits: Cover © George Ancona/International Stock; p. 4 © Steve Satushek/Image Bank; pp. 7, 20 © Jack Kurtz/Impact Visuals; p. 8 © Scott Thode/International Stock; p. 11 © Patrick Ramsey/International Stock; p. 12 © Orion/International Stock; p. 15 © Hoa-Qui/Liaison International; p. 16 © Rod Low; p. 19 © Ira Lipsky/International Stock.

Quinn, Daniel P.
   I am Buddhist / Daniel P. Quinn
      p.   cm. — (Religions of the world)
   Includes index.
   Summary: A young Chinese boy living in San Francisco with his family describes the principles and ceremonies of Buddhism.
   ISBN 0-8239-2379-7
   1. Buddhism—Juvenile literature. [1. Buddhism.] I. Series: Religions of the world (Rosen Publishing Group)
BQ4032.Q5 1996
294.3—dc20
                                          96-6978
                                          CIP
                                          AC

Manufactured in the United States of America

Contents

47-530

Being Buddhist

My name is Yuyen. I live in San Francisco. I am a Chinese Buddhist. There are many different kinds of Buddhism. But all Buddhists are followers of the Buddha, which means "the **enlightened** (en-LY-tend) one." Enlightenment is the complete understanding of the world and of life and of your place in life. We believe that the Buddha understood all of these things. We try to become enlightened by following the Buddha's teachings.

◀ From the time they are children, Buddhists follow the Buddha's teachings.

5

Prayer

My mother and father pray to the Buddha. They teach me to say prayers that help us tell the Buddha our needs and ask for his blessings. My parents taught me that prayer helps us to be closer to the Buddha. Prayer also helps us understand the teachings of the Buddha. The teachings of the Buddha help us understand life.

Sometimes Buddhists pray at home. Other times they pray in a temple. ▶

Refuge in the Buddha

We learn to take **refuge** (REF-youj) in the examples the Buddha set during his life—the things he said and the things he did. "Taking refuge" means receiving protection, comfort, and care. We get all of these things when we try to live our lives the way that the Buddha did. Taking refuge in the Buddha is the first of what my father calls the three jewels.

◀ Buddhists carry out the teachings of the Buddha in part by caring for others.

Refuge in the Dharma

The second jewel is taking refuge in the **Dharma** (DAR-ma). The Dharma means the teachings of the Buddha. It also means other things: duty, goodness, rules, and truth. My father says we take refuge in the Dharma after we take refuge in the Buddha. This means that we take refuge in the Buddha's teachings as well as in the examples he set during his life. We learn to care for others, to do good things, to follow rules, and to be honest.

One good thing a Buddhist may do is to ▶ spend time with an elderly neighbor.

Refuge in the Sangha

The third jewel is taking refuge in the Sangha. Sangha is our **commitment** (kom-MIT-mint) to our community, the people around us. In order to show our commitment, we try to follow **precepts** (PREE-septs). Three of these precepts are that we do not destroy life, we do not steal, and we live a **moral** (MORE-ul) life.

◄ Buddhists learn that all living things are important.

Karma

Karma (KAR-muh) means that every action has an effect. The law of karma says that if I do something good, something good will happen to me. My mother says that we live many lives. Everything that we do and say has an effect on each of our lives. My mother says that we should always try to be loving and kind. She says that this will bring good things to us in this life and in future lives.

All Buddhists believe in karma. This little girl is a Buddhist from Thailand. ▶

Guan Yin

Guan Yin (GWAN yin) is a very important goddess. She is called the "Goddess of Mercy (MUR-see)." My mother says that she is the perfect example of mercy and love. She helps us become enlightened, as the Buddha was. She also saves people from trouble, such as fire and sickness. We have a statue of Guan Yin in our house. We honor (ON-ur) her and pray to her every morning.

◀ Guan Yin is important to all Buddhists.
This statue of her is in Japan.

Buddha Day

Buddha Day is a very special day for us. It is the day we celebrate the birth of the Buddha. It is the day, when he was older, that he became enlightened. It is also the day he died many years later. My family puts a statue of the baby Buddha in a bowl. We put flowers over the statue. We pour perfumed water or tea over the baby Buddha. It is a very happy time.

There are statues of the Buddha all over the world. This statue is in Taiwan. ▶

Honoring the Ancestors

My father and mother have taught me that it is important to honor our **ancestors** (AN-ses-torz). Ancestors are the relatives who have lived before us, such as our grandparents and great-grandparents. On special days, we light **incense** (IN-sents) in front of a picture of my grandparents. We leave treats of rice cakes in front of the picture. We also sing special songs and pray.

◀ One way Buddhists honor their ancestors is by lighting prayer sticks.

The Sutras

There are many stories about the Buddha and his life. The books that tell about the Buddha are called **sutras** (SOO-truz). The stories tell us about what the Buddha taught and how he lived. They tell the story of how he came to understand the meaning of life. We use parts of the sutras as prayers. We also learn from them.

Glossary

ancestor (AN-ses-tor) Relatives who lived before you.

commitment (kom-MIT-mint) Pledge or promise.

Dharma (DAR-ma) Teachings of the Buddha.

enlightened (en-LY-tend) Having spiritual understanding.

Guan Yin (GWAN yin) Goddess of Mercy.

honor (ON-ur) Pay respect or praise to.

incense (IN-sents) Spice or scent that is burned.

karma (KAR-muh) Every action having an effect.

mercy (MUR-see) Compassion.

moral (MORE-ul) Good, positive.

precept (PREE-sept) Law.

refuge (REF-youj) Shelter, comfort, safety.

sutras (SOO-truz) Books that describe the Buddha
    and his life.

Index